Matter

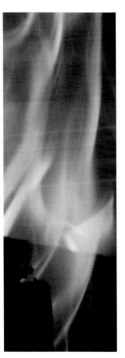

All things are matter. Matter is things you can see and feel.

Matter is things you cannot see too – such as air.

Matter can be a solid,
a liquid or a gas.

Solids

A rubber duck is a solid.

This car is a solid.

This wooden chair is a solid.

A muffin is a solid.

Liquids

This liquid fills the jug.

 Oil is a liquid.

Rain is a liquid.

Gases

Air is a gas.

This is a gas.

Gas fills this balloon.

Liquids can turn into solids if they cool down.

This solid can
turn into a liquid.

Now, you have a turn!

Is it a solid, a liquid or a gas?

Matter matters to me and you.

Words to blend

matter	rubber	hotter
air	chair	car
oil	down	turn
cannot	solid	liquid
cool	now	wooden
balloon	muffin	duck
gas	things	feels

Before reading

Synopsis: Matter can be a liquid, a solid or a gas. Can you tell which matter is which?

Review graphemes/phonemes: ar or ur ow oi ear air ure er

Book discussion: Look at the cover and read the title together. Check that children understand that *matter* can mean a substance. Everything on Earth is made of some sort of matter. Matter includes invisible gases as well as solids and liquids.

Link to prior learning: Display the graphemes ar, ur, ow, oi, air, ure, er. Ask children to read each grapheme out loud. Can they think of a word that uses each grapheme? Write some of their suggested words and practise reading them.

Vocabulary check: solid – something that keeps it shape

Decoding practice: Turn to pages 2–3 and see how quickly children can find and read a word with each of the graphemes *er, ee, oo, air*.

Tricky word practice: Display the word *they* and ask children to circle the tricky part of the word (*ey*, which makes a long /ai/ sound). Practise writing and reading this word.

After reading

Apply learning: Ask: *Can you name at least one solid, one liquid and one gas?* (Encourage children to look back at the book if they need help with this.)

Comprehension

- Can solids become liquids?
- Can you think of any liquids that aren't in the book?
- If solids can become liquids, do you think liquids can become solids? How?

Fluency

- Pick a page that most of the group read quite easily. Ask them to reread it with pace and expression. Model how to do this if necessary.
- Ask children to choose a favourite page and read it with appropriate expression and intonation.
- Practise reading the words on page 17.

Tricky words review

all	are	you
and	be	the
into	they	have
to	me	so
old	do	there